Inverse Sky

KUHL HOUSE POETS

edited by Mark Levine & Ben Doller

POEMS BY JOHN ISLES

UNIVERSITY OF IOWA PRESS, IOWA CITY

Inverse Sky

University of Iowa Press, Iowa City 52242

Copyright © 2008 by John Isles

www.uiowapress.org

Printed in the United States of America

Design by Richard Hendel

The University of Iowa Press is a member of Green Press Initiative
and is committed to preserving natural resources.

Printed on acid-free paper

Library of Congress Cataloging-in-Publication Data

Isles, John.

    Inverse sky: poems / by John Isles.

        p.   cm.—(Kuhl House poets)

ISBN-13: 978-1-58729-686-4 (pbk.)

ISBN-10: 1-58729-686-1 (pbk.)

I. Title.   2008009628

PS3609.S58158 2008

811'.6—dc22

08 09 10 11 12 P 5 4 3 2 1

for Kristen

Contents

Acknowledgments

Thanks to the editors and readers of the following magazines in which some of these poems first appeared, sometimes in different forms: *American Letters and Commentary, Boston Review, Colorado Review, Denver Quarterly, Electronic Poetry Review, Los Angeles Review, New Orleans Review, Pleiades,* and *Pool.*

"Desperate Tender" was awarded the Ruskin Art Club Prize from the *Los Angeles Review.*

Many thanks also to the friends who read this book in manuscript form and offered insights and suggestions that made a tremendous difference: Lary Kleeman, Joseph Lease, D. A. Powell, and Mary Wang. Finally, thanks to the series editors, Mark Levine and Ben Doller, who showed a great amount of faith and made many invaluable suggestions.

This book was nudged into its beginnings with the help of a grant from the National Endowment of the Arts. Many thanks to that organization and its readers.

1

From the charred remains of the Vision Fire — *we see*

As we believe — a green scar implicating us in earthly affairs

Green land grab of coyote bush and cow parsnip

Flourishing without vengeance where Paradise Estates once stood

Bishop pine growing into conflagrations

Cones detonating from sealed pitch — exploding shells

Seeds tearing open ground in a bright wound —

We were driving, sucked in by the ocean's breath

Into clouds and crowds of salt-slaked pine

Green burned in us — tourist dollars

Wolves to the flock, realtors to the vista point —

We were talking — words were waters in far-off deserts

Falling into oil fires, indiscriminately

We were looking — trees grew intricate in passages of the brain

We imagined being — before we were —

In briny intertidal zones — pliant among rushes

Whelmed with light spent in the estranged light of day

Putting the Bird Back in the Sky

Here I am —

of two minds: all eyes — all ears — for an echo.

Driving into the sunset,
who is not gold and mining? Who is not a piece of one,
son-like in that way?

I call you mine and I am yours.

The tree lover becomes a tree, wooden and breathing
in reverse, giving my livelihood away.
Green and leafing canopy for the herd, I wear
leaves with my skin,

tear them off with my eyes.

A bird flies over and I am birdbrained
and precocious, flying before my time.
I marry a bird, swallow it for its song, the vibrations

singing *I am*. The bird and its flying,
small-time creators, leave me with nothing
to stake a life on.

I have no choice.

In the sun too much, charioteer and burning
in my father's shoes, I call the whistling air —

The glass doors open and what was free
for eyes isn't free anymore . . .

Part common daisy, part mountain,
Shasta daisies in hybrid wizardry awaken in sunlight —
like advertisements for themselves displayed
before a panoramic landscape of painterly hills
and a gold-strewn stream no one will ever pan.

               And here I am, grafting —
balled into a bruise outside the hospital, overlooking
the humantide ebbing into the sunset

                                in a picture show
I've seen too many times, the dialogue
on my lips entirely wrong for the occasion —

-a woman on a cell, her voice lingering — briefly
-a stooped man waving, the traffic not stopping

Junipero Serra, congealed into stone,
looks down . . .   He points westerly and away
from the convalescing flowers, toward

the Pacific opening a window in the fog.

The globe shrinks to the size of a throbbing head,
hangs at the lip of that diner darling,
the worldly skirt behind the counter.
Righteous and undeserving next to a Coca-Cola bottle
and escaping gasses, treelike and evanescent.
The forested air! In a wake of hormonal perfume:
drained air, fly-daze. Swinging door of the mind
closing, opening: momentum's obsession.
Dust unsettling, the stranger dust.

A gun in the hand adds to the possibilities.
A gun in the hand in the Hollywood version
is a sometimes song of one who vanished.
Sometimes flies, granted brief reprieve from gravity.
Stubby pines enduring the real estate they will become.
Sometimes sirens — jagged profusions dismantling . . .
A river of shadows, the body runs into a personal shore —
broken bottles smoothed into uninhabitable shells.
Home is over. Lay your head down.

I'd live a lie and tell it too.
This one for you, this for the girl next door
in a film about a film and a starlet
so hayseed she could change the world.
Her desperation and dye job, my derby
and debonair, my dimestore dalliance.
Limelight stand-in for moonlight, I want you
MaryJane and pigtails, I call you Peaches.
Long arm of snow-white. Warm-blooded wonderland.
I call you Iowa or Idaho, farm girl and manqué.
Manqué mostly: that potential rendezvous
you've known all your life, my interlocutor —
my girl is yours, at the center of intrigue.
Authorities raising alarms, authorities giving chase
into dimly lit mansions of swank smoke rings.
A sleuth in the shadows, a lambing in the corner
of every illicit room and everything you don't say
can be used against you in a catty gossip column.
It's a highball charade, a swimming pool
the size of *in the swim of things.*
As in the beginning, the body filmed from below,
pressing into the sky, as in the end, coppers
gathered around the kid on the way up, the author
on the way down, embracing the surface.

leaves fall from the sky
as lovely lies for the first time every time.

In the bloodlust exchange, two reds for every yellow.
Every breath's a fair trade in the skin of the world.
The streets, this peopled street and green logo paper cups
attended by hunting hands . . .

My how many skies of the gone world,
outside the museum's diorama,
lives in a state of inner nationhood:
Redwood in the clear cutting,
tongue in mine I cannot learn — rattler glottis —
tick and hum of the nonnegotiable hunger.

Where my eyes would plant their flag
my people would root and be your people . . .

A mariposa cloud menaces a hostile sun.
One lodges in an ear that cannot hear a thing:

Beauty's aggression —

whiting over a river's white sound,
a drowning — baptism of forgetfulness.

Trees at the end of the day lift their common skirt
along the avenue: world flesh sigh in summer stagnation.

Sunlight stripped of its edges — chimera of colors
roiling. Pale-burning grasses, pot o' gold oranges —

streetwise and errant sunset of a munibus —
ocean under too much pressure, trying to escape itself —
lake of eyes in the window-flash.

Pigeons launch from St. Leo's and the ringing dark iron —
trading one form for another — to wild the call.
Vacate the Catholic air. Figure feathered flesh there.
Eavesdrop in the wired space of telephone poles.

A hawk into the pigeon confusion —
the alarm below, mounting into a consensual look.

A face in the faces.
                        A girl's name finds a home
in a botched tattoo job, the arm jerking into the crowd.

Imported trees, imperturbed, maintain a social distance.
Irises turn geisha fashion — their silky ciliated throats —

open to every sliver of light, every body.

My Comfortress of Unsuccess

(Mary Austen)

Named all the birds without a gun.
Shot looks sidelong without a glance.
A glinting, a white dress —
I live in the sun's drunken vaquero state.

I had to be a girl. Appendage to a mule,
distant daughter of some bad Indian.
Scorpion skittering into a raw skull.
That mineral night, depthless black sky.

Nightsinging mockingbirds oscillate
at man-height, build palaces in viscid foliage.
A burial squad pecks for blind water.
From the choked maw of noon, an all-time-cry.

A girl, a dust cloud and letters
traveling through sand ablutions.
My mesquite valley drifting away,
its dry fingering of my throat — wild civility

This is devastation, this is a walk in the ruins
where I would find you, my sun in the east,
penetrating eye in a blinding dust cloud.
(This is just a test.)

I find — my sleek and evasive. Water-skin in the humidity.
Forcefield of surface that calls no name.
Saboteur-cry: Tentative notch in the condor project.
Methinks I am no bigger than my head.

Fish and frenzy in my old Buick, fins and free-spawning,
I've come to the hush of Gothic cacti — candelabras gone wild.
To this private ground. Rose in a time-lapsed nature film.
(This is the countdown that never ends.)

You think if nothing happens nothing is destroyed?
Rub two together and look the other way:
I'm detonation-sized in the horizon,
a probability in space.

A particle when you pay attention to me.
Walking out of desert, dissipating in the atmosphere.
The blue of my thinking broken through,
alone is — *nearer to thee.* And farther, too.

I sail, I go by water, aloof and navicular,
a shipwreck, or a ship that weighed anchor,
that moved on, the hours logged five hundred miles
from here in a place just like this one.
Because going forth is going in circles:
This world is all the worlds there are. Because:
Money. Tallies in a ledger, provisions,
and expenses, half-lost meanderings, the discoveries
of half-truths, the course chartered in black ink.
Bird just like the old country bird.
Innovations of trees, palm and palimpsest.
The probable voyage, the possible bay
in the town where a band marches in a wind
that drove ship to shore a hundred lifetimes ago.
Students wave their spirit flags, teachers
in the aisles bristle at *the natives getting restless.*
Players hurl themselves to no end.
In a rush of steel and victory, the crowd
rises, exits the parking lot.

To succumb to the fleshly stream of the crowd
trafficking in the equivocal light of this sea-girt place.

To keep oneself a stranger and a pilgrim.

Vestige of fishermen long gone,
tourist among charlatans and ten-cent emotions
of the Ripley's Arcade. Silver and pixilated,

Robot Man dances in a mechanized delirium.
Coins travel their solitary ways in the penny arcades.

To lurk in the diversions of five minutes ago —
worlds in passing — always and nowhere going fast.
The ink of this ilk turns back and circles

in a blue snow of the interior, in needling tracks,
the thousand junctures where hunger and chaos
meet in theory, meet in practice.

To spiral loosely around a certain stony bench,
in an uncertain perfume somebody left behind.

The shape of her coming to mind in evening's bustle:

The opening mouth, the suggestive evaporation.

This way into the dark,

                                 this agent
of darkness and its theater. Outside:

Gull-glide and gaudy glare in maritime air,
a study in the stasis of moving things.

The tide pulling and pulling

reveals the liquid state of every thing.

                        A girl trails a fingernail
across her boyfriend's cheek, the two loose limbed,
draped across a bench, a look of cool boredom —

their talk secretive over willing waves —

                                    the current

whisks a Styrofoam cup, a city of ebullient feeder fish —

out the channel, into privacy chambers of the deep.

Cosmos

My closing eyes find them in the dark,
my eyes that can't see anything like to make things up:

Jackhammers chipping away at the cosmos next door,
the world so light it drifts in and out of my thoughts.

Being stardust and radio waves in empty space,
the workers listen in their parallel universe to a radio

beyond their hammering. Like clocks. Like fists
pounding at the door, an earthly music of the spheres —

same old "Blue Bayou," different silver moon.
Their luna — my evening tide — tugging at the water's body.

All morning I've been trying to yank from my skin
a *cantora* so supple she bends me in two.

The cosmos bustle with frightened space —
then there are neighbors in all their neighborhoods,

their starry blossoms promising more than
tomatoes in stilted orbits flopping down:

a promise, a force poised and ready for the next move
there in conceptual space — and here on earth.

The city burning down, the city burning up.
Rubble rearranged into towers with lathe frames.
Flame the multitude dreams — no. Not these *bodies*
a hundred years after — carried by escalators
into daylight, still world of unwavering walls.

City of one — cowlicked and lumbering, sea sucked
on Market Street, overboard in auriferous wonder.
City of divergent narratives spied from a wave-swept
schooner — in a tundra gaze of lusty waves —
white wolves in the conforming element.

Crowd of one's attention in which a woodsman from Oregon
plays the American in an English movie set in France —
accents hard to place, smart scarves in a studio breeze.

City of conflicting desires, passing girl in whose eyes
hurricanes germinate. Gaze arcing from the wharf
to the come-hither gull-glide. As a maiden into a cloud

of mayflies — *Marry I will, Marry I will* —
swallowed by the assembly around a portable mountain.

The city of climbers threading an atmospheric eye.

2

The Uncertainty Pastoral

Tall white desire, button down unbuttoned

Impulse purchase in the checkout aisle

Breath mint where the breath was

Where the republic perishes —

This life is a mist, a cloud in the making

Glass of water on a hill — head steaming off

Voluptuous water — like that — drop of

Lead like that in the fat tissue —

Only a man harrowing clouds

A man breaking things with closed eyes

In desert distances — a nobody

Insurgency of sands over time

Explosive device — singed seed

Sapling competing for a place in the clear cutting

Bounded water — startled out of itself

1

There's nothing I wouldn't do. I'd be sheer. Discretionary purchase.
Water and silk, shiny car and a smoke you would inhale, you would
blow into the parking lot. But I'm destroyed. I'm under your radar,
some body under the overpass, talking to himself. I'm inconceivable
to wanton summer air, like a tree. It's hormonal, it's subliminal,
call me home:

2
Brick and glass,

a steeple stopped by an inverse of sky —

handful of dust . . .

This street receding into a lesser shade of itself,

running parallel to the first person streetwise narrative —

"I alone of all mankind."

3
But soft. What light.
And there's no going in.

The fog landlocking St. Mary's
disperses into the Oakland hills,
the light losing and slanting the property values.

If I could wear it with my skin,
an inside on the outside worn,
tongue in the ache . . .

4

Night heaves: hot breaths
breaking in the runaway dark
and bottle brush trees following me home,

sticky in the bosom of the air —
sweetly coursing in my sick blood.

Night and birds singing,
that I might touch . . .

"In the sweat of thy face."

5

That close. To what? The very traffic.
Gasoline gone vapor. Exhaust

over the Asian market, the slender
shoots, fruits and exotica — here

in the city of *just passing through*

it's not *beautiful hallucinatory haze,*
not *celestial skyline*. It's Construction Site:

6

Timber relenting, timber stacked. It's Crocker Mansion:
Song of the self-made man: "Dig here."

For the heads angling in a skyward boardroom,
it's high-rise vertigo:

land equals green gold, water equals white gold.

7

I'd be the end   of the endless ocean —
be the beginning too   and the opening

in the bounce   of your blouse . . .

Be somebody   else   his hairstyle

his pretty soul   in the self-help aisle.

A body   capitulating to the poem
you are   the poem I'd be.

A private hell   a not even that —

a face in the faces —   metallic shine —
Mary-glow —   always other —

Green gold for white gold   burning oil

Dark Pastoral

The lights went out
The secretaries forgot to put truth in the water
Executive orders snowing down on the industrial park —
Kerfuffle in the money matter —
Redundancy sparkles in the marketplace
And we in purest indifference look miles deep
Pinkish flowers and ants we stepped on along the way
The tiny lights —

Let's count backwards from eternity
Under a tree, in the shade dissembling
Let's wander out of the poem, into the fog
Muzzling the bridge between us and them —
The leadership — setting the wheels in motion
Only where's the car, where's the road —
Where are you for that matter?
I don't want you walking the side of the interstate
They haven't gotten around to, they keep talking up —

The truth went out
Wandering burnt hills in the pitch
With reeds in its pockets, a herd for the hoarding
Word goes out — it's all over
I've been looking for you all over
I was driving, talking to myself
Could somebody just pick up the phone?
Could somebody reach a hand into the machine —

Then the earth — its birds and verdure
bored me, bore into me . . .
I looked into calculated distances —

called them *you,* you who bring out
the white-boy stiff in me, broken down
straggler on Jericho Turnpike in me.

There's McDonald's, there's Wendy's,
the boarded hulk of the roller rink,
center of excessive kissing, cherry scented

lipgloss — Jordache and Calvin Klein —
room robbed of oxygen — pressured sub-

marine plunge; — and the bends.

Transmissions whining, boys in monster
trucks spewing up the beach . . .

Electric guitars hijack the darkness.

Night upon night I have walked —
thatched briar and thistle-whipped and everywhere

there is not an amber field.

Everywhere the sun consumed,
surf hissing behind the scenes,

heavy metal in the parking lot —

In the first conception of hell
I travel the round earth's flat orthodoxy —
scrub oak and pitch pine —

scrawny deer some hunters left
to its own devices —
to take the lie of lime and die

on fastidious lawns of the fashionable.

They're having a lawn party —
the man from the *Times* on hand —
they're decked out in summer whites

and Canada geese take the invitation
that wasn't given — it's all scat and skidaddle —

piss and moan and wings
into the infra-red sunset, my dear

infra-human, I

Say goodbye to the rearranging waters,
say *you* to atmospheric contingencies —

the dark — the darker — institutions

of cruelty; people never but machinery
always and ever onward —

alien-eyed tractor in a fog —
somebody's driving, nobody's in charge.

Rain in mud, sloppy mouths —
sucking sounds of ten thousand steps,

and nobody walking

where the sun would unclothe itself . . .

The lick the linger in the undergrowth,

the animal lurking the animal wants out.

In the umpteenth conception of hell . . .

In a desert of the east . . .

seven years of plenty followed by seven years
of the sun's redundancy . . .

There comes a time to come undone,
to come and go in a single breath.

To brave the green-filmed water,
drift in pungent chemical decay

past eelgrass edged periphery —

broken glass
                        screeching tires —

There comes a time to enter the world
without you, without hope,

and love the things not loving back.

Notes toward a Social Realism

[sketch of motel alienated in neon]

I am here — and there too
                    in the world

watching as a man lurches into the breech

with a shopping cart

derelict sun having set on a motel pool

resembling an oozy creek rainbow streaked,
reassembling in halogen haloes in sundry luke-blue.

A car alarm engages a neighborhood dog
in its fenced-in yard: Everywhere,

the whimpering.

[no marshland for miles]

Night-herons fly reconnaissance sorties for . . .
some lost water

                    grasses and their children . . .
page upon page in the library of waters.

[vacancy]

        A shadowed man-shape wheels
into the tree-lined boulevard and into the spotlight

of motion detectors in a dumpster alley

a city that recycles

And suddenly sycamores, flustered by black birds
and their love cries . . . many many

in red vacancy light

Sidereal Messengers

In skyscraper grasses —

                                the insect eyes,

numbers I cannot gather into a number —

world I am nature to.

Anglers at my mouth, I am disappearing even now,
abandoned toy useless in the weeds:

What patrol cars find in the wake of a violent crime —
a man behind Safeway with a knowledge too certain,

helicopters chopping the air into sound bites —

And the grassy-haired, green-eyed shock of joy
I would die for . . .

Bumper-sticker adage to . . .
                           dim for,

curl into the loosening place of skin and flowerbeds and sleep —

vehicle, subject of
rational forces, the dehumanized face —

                                    millions of faces:

Ladybugs rising from picnics in the grass.
Ladybugs abducted by the whim of convection currents,

hot air rising — adherence to the laws

                              — passionate wings,

a five hundred mile vacuum suck

into the Sierra Nevada.

They settle down in a slumber party,
a tower of sexual somnambulism —

that treasure of,
that black-suited void, with its department of planets,

its insect subsidiaries —

children of urgent traffic — engining into

June and stars at the tip of nobody's tongue.

Gospel, According to This Very Moment

Time for me to start leaving the words out

Time for you to start putting them back in

All the names falling from you like arrows

Eros rearranging in *deserts of vast eternity*

Every pore — seething with instant fire

I emerge from zero — human — and there you are

Window — body — fleshly field

I could call you *unbearable nearness of the bride*

Room of tongues you would talk me into

Birdly flame tearing open the fabric of this

Rectangle of the neighbor's yard growing — out of view

The trees keep being "the trees" — water — keeps going

Flies hover in neutral air-space

The sound, a cloth of anesthesia, saturating the day

Dimming in dusk's blanket amnesia —

Sleeper, who is not an arrow in a god-bow?

3

The Arcadia Negotiations

Cherry tree, if I held you close, where would we be?
The body where I was born is less than liquid,
less than the stories the fathers told.

Sun-stunned water in a pink stain — mid-air.
Bleeding without blood. *Sweet mouth.*

Grassy cutting sounds — like water parting —
insects carry on in a torn world.

Cherry tree, when I was a boy, a girl, minefield of skin,
I walked into this stranger's coastline — impenetrable deep sky,

medicinal trees, the bay unhinged — salt, sulfur —
too rich to breathe —

                    Is it any wonder —
molested by the air like you — I hack away,

sprout a smeared version behind the eyes?

Something there is
that will not let us be —

fire zones in brownhill outskirts, festive flags
of the used car lot, shine like blood in the traffic surge.

Bodies pulse out of shops — Juanita's,
El Ojo de Agua — into a larger body of people.

The boulevard trails off into heat-choked hills,
coyotes camouflaged in quivering manzanita —
conference of quail —

After the Mexican War,
Vallejo surrenders to the Bear Flag Republic.
The mission burning and he is serving

wine and eggs and chorizo to the Americans
who have come to arrest him. It is time
to move on — higher ground, or lower ground.

Good or gone, roulette of beget and beyond,
redwood groves over hills, simple trade

of light for air, vertical for vertiginous.

Westerly, wind —
dry cough at the foot of — the immensity of . . .
the Pacific continuing in the expansive mode —

myself — in the diminishing state of sleeplessness —
dissolving song — carny tune in a palmy district.
Desert of one — down sidewalks buried in the drift —

maritime atmospheres in the tourist talk —
bygone schooner under the unforgiving heft of high-rises.

Traffic swells from the broken backbone of the road.

The world is dead behind us —
canoes gliding past forests of skeletal trees,

vague weathers of selves and salvages —
ocean pouring into more ocean.

Waking into summer fog — water flowers can't drink!

I am intermingled and cannot distinguish
the skin's sensations from the world.

This view allows a tree trunk, bougainvillea
sexing up the neighbor's stairs, burgundy

clouds fast forwarding into the field
you make in this regard — claim on what is

true, entity like zero — chasm — as far as the eye
can see:

Zero's bride —

fog smothering its landlocked lover,
the Pacific rising up to overthrow

solidity: soft-maidenly at your window —
sigh in a sieve, sweat on green water.

Prowling beach grass in withering summer —
it whites out faces in the sidewalk flow,

buries the Farrallones in thickening zero —
pulling you into darker thoughts —

smoke from no one's mouth fills and erases,

fills and erases (you)

Voices, voices . . .
ambient in the neighborhood —

Who is it this time?

Polk and Santa Anna skirting the border,
playing out private storms in nation building light?

Listen my heart —
Dead August: flies don't budge, leaves don't stir —

nothing happening, nothing *ever* happening —
The plum tree filling too quickly here,

emptying too quickly — *sheisse* plums.
Nobody eats the things.

After the *Invasión Yanqui* the Senator from Illinois
wants to know who will show him the American soil
stained with American blood . . .

Dead August, nothing is still happening.
Branches impart deciduous ways to birds
in their reaches — birdly spirit of light,

the still world in interstices, city carved out
by a city of branches.

Vertical for vicissitudes

Inward awe for a city of transfers and promotions

For winter-seeming summer nights

Dull sublunary lovers

Pleasures like yesterday's news

For a blasted field stretching from gray to gray

Crumbling concrete, dirty birds, interminable fog

— Not doves throating gossip to the gods,
but scrub jays, blue torches in an empty lot.

The Pacific reaching out of its water compartments
delivers pelagic distances

into the opossum light of public haunts —
chalk outlines of lives dreamed by the waterfront.

The tide lifts *any* body. We could —

if we had a lighthouse for a match light,
a house of water for a house of debt . . .

We could sleep here.

I forget my country, breaking into pieces —
the recently elected — branches downed in a gust —
monarchs unclotting — frenzied in the yard.

The others sleep in their separate rooms —
the boy dreams of monkeys hogging all the cakes.
You are blinded at the foot of a lighthouse —

waves thick and sweet with algae,
something imminent in the distance.
What goes unexpressed between us.

Glaring shore and an expectation of water
where there is none — in the long white

of your throat and yes your eyes from here
are transparent, your face a cloud —

please tell me again what does the fog say —

4

The Next Loneliness

TV static where the window was —

Heat waves — the horizon like a tree — yellowing

Palpable air, sweet throated birdless air

You could crush with too much loving

It begins with a war *we* are not fighting, bodies coming — home —
nonetheless in body bags, empty in *Time*'s photographs.

In the chlorinated clarity of swimming pools.

Among diapers, sleeping pills, plastic bins —

things to hold other things in a sea of

the oil stained, littered — the unrelenting parking lot.

Empty except for the unforgiven one, suicidal, homicidal,
who could be you — *you* could have nowhere to go —

Don't you have nowhere to go?

Try to be serious, intelligent, going places . . .

But you're asphyxiated in this light, this smog, the tremendous
bodies, the absolute crap people buy —

Let's start over.

Let's take a breath —

Begin with a holly tree, ripe with berries —
cherry ripe — berries birds don't eat.

We could include the palm trees of postcard California,
put the oak back in Oakland, go *there* —

to leaf legions the children kick up,

their heads inside a haiku, the distance
through trees/ neighbor stepping out/

from a cloud of leaves.

Begin with the garden in their faces — cherry ripe!

Smoky exhaust from their moving mouths,
the transparent bag of the world

inflating —

I Know If I Find You I Will Have to Leave the Earth

For Drew

1

Ferried light

Vehicular gleam

Tourist tread and storefront windows

Shattered light, angled light

Pooling in a passenger's eye —

2

                              You —

not *you* exactly — a sip and a headful,
drip of light, liquid green, leaves

turning up their undersides
like dresses —

you wanted to be brash waves in sunlight.

Not paperwork, a body requisitioned,
not flowing in proper channels.

Not deranged burning jungles.
Not desert spaces of your brain,

or the parade of faces — broken light
reassembled in the TV screen —

sleek like new cars — languishing.

Not advertisements for the dead.

3
And I went and told it to the residue.

4
I am small, teach me to be smaller:
when I was a grownup there were lessons
in running, in walking, this is me crawling.

I lived with the others in a town
the size of myself, requisite rowboats
tethered to moorings. Winters we pulled

them from sulfur mud, blackening green seaweed —
half the world attached. Dumpyard gulls
disappeared in the sinking white sky.

Their black throated cries galled our days,
crazed krill in broad swaths of industry.

5
Could've been the way the shadows.

Could've been devotion.

Trick of light, antiqued air, crizzled glass —

How is it the car keeps driving —

6
As if it could matter,
as if it had to do with you. —

A taste of salt, too fine for the eye,
vague humidity —
warm-damp against the skin

where there was skin
and where there wasn't —
the world reeled the way of

sand gathered round aggressive grasses,

seeds loosened into —
everything moving — and the world,

the wind —

switched on.

For the World's Great Economies

You could call and listen

Press zero for a human being

And the NSA triangulates our voices

In the communication stream

Michael is saying — he is the one I called

"The homeless guy" for a while — my student

He is saying he could have hugged his teacher — who wasn't me

After the heart attack, after the right word rightly given

The heart fights back

"Appropriate" didn't seem so

I wanted him to see my broken —

Wanted broken to open

The Hunger

Smoke of my own breath —
                    signature
                              not wholly/ mine.

Shine sheering off the edges of things —

summer swallowed like sugar —
powdered, blowing into the blue/ the American   sky.

You retreat into yourself, into the closed rooms
of your loverliness, my lubberliness,

the movement of your hands a sweetened speech.

Tousled hair, frazzled eyes —
in your after work distress you are frozen in glass; —

one who is equal to this one-liness in a bareness
of multitudes, the crowd, the crowd in oblivion of skin,

Oakland's gray scale warehouses walling in the estuary,
where Jack London paddled his way/ — out.

A freighter disengages from the concrete pier,
a dream of arctic expanses, call of —

Freighter in all probability zeroing in
on the next load to feed this —

Sharp elbow'd city.

Apple blossom city.

City of hunger.

Every thing tastes of us.

Wind through the sieve of you and up the boulevard,
wind that is more equal than you, that will not

sail you into the unobtainable reaches of real estate.

Salt air from the bay veiling the incendiary hills,
unveiling the liquid,
                    the gaseous state

of solid matter —

                    It reaches
into grasses alive in your moving

like a flag, tearing into autumn —

down a string of events,
each a theory in the making —

version of my sleepless state,
cloistered cell enlarging loneliness:

Battered night heron in the schoolyard,
uninvited, inevitable,

night vision briefly granted,
drift of snow —
hospital bed extending   sharp wings,

or dull knives into smoke
                    and less than smoke —

dark startling,
                    the dark matter

is new again —

Evangelical Economics

Yes we're buying yes who could afford not to.

Yes we are relaxing to the music
piped out to the sidewalk, admiring the prices,

pure products in the windows undressing,
cicadas sloganeering in the trees, infesting

the summer campaign, burrowing into and into . . .

Yes the beautiful detonation on the horizon,
the sun become less mechanical in nature.

It is all music to die to, to keep dying to
because we are *fine* because everyone is.

And here we are, counting pennies —

One is always climbing [Lord]

How many to summit the monetary mountain.
How many to sleep in foiled clouds.

To live the life of roadside castaway
flowers sucking color from the air

in the city that will not have us,
city of glass structures looming lightly as holograms.

One is climbing, two is scuttling down [Lord]

We two ruminating money in and money out,
the everlasting figure equivalent to I into you,

the division we are, a number approximating
the cicada eggs in a square mile of Jersey woods,

or the number of stars in the milky way.

Diorama with a 20-Watt Bulb Inside

Child hunkered down in grass,
breaking it for letters.

"Here's T," he says, "here's I"
— stalling in the parking lot.

Sharks can't get you on land,
the father voice goes.

And the child:
"On *Scooby Doo,* they do, they do."

I turn to take him in —
he is shepherding ants into a bath

they don't exactly want.
The three worlds of us. *Lambs.*

Simply a matter of going over the bluff —
everything really — and everything else

adrift in international waters.

And When I Waked I Cried to Dream Again

1

Smashed glass   white splintering

greater waters   from the lesser

trace in the air   gust

someone leaving   a door open

hole in the world   anyone

falls into

2

Small again, kosmos again —

my tender terror in thickening distance,
playing in the scribble-scrabble —

instructing the ocean where to flow
in its cold war of water versus water.

Choosing or chosen for this moment —

the call to paralysis —
a taste, molecule by molecule shaping

in the corners of his round mouth —

the sea becoming the sea —

3
The land, dead in its pores all the war long — glossed by fog.

4
Waves get down on their knees,
gulls strafe a boat in the channel —

a fisherman trawling habitually for dying breeds

sweeps vacant shells away;
it looks easy — other lives usually do.

The boy returns debris to the four-year-old sea —

crab shells, egg sacs, Styrofoam — pieces of —

on the way out, the way in.

Whirls of thinking as he navigates the jetty.

5
Worlds to go, sleepy sea-stained worlds.

Whatever I said I was
was blown youth, delirious smoke in the woods

where the boy had been.
Wet-dark, chameleon's dish, in the sheets

where the mouth had been,
the data into circuitry — her face her eyes

"her spittle . . . life's own fount to me."
The data out: *let me be your new and improved.*

Where the words had been,
the seventeen-year-old atmosphere squeezed,

my mouth unhinged northwesterly,
the shine and steam of the carwash became me.

From the soap scudded interior, I surfaced
and nothing was the matter, people scurried

with vacuums; my loneliness populated!
And it was good. It was *progress.*

And I walked up and down upon my own skin.
And I never returned.

The first two lines of "Dark Pastoral" were extracted from an opinion piece by Lewis Lapham in *Harper's Magazine.*

The title "I Know If I Find You I Will Have to Leave the Earth" is from A. R. Ammons's poem "Hymn."

"Diorama with a 20-Watt Bulb Inside" is adapted from a phrase in Donald Revell's essay "Invisible Green II."

Section 3 of "And When I Waked I Cried to Dream Again" is adapted from a line by Nathaniel Tarn in his poem "The Great Odor of Summer."

Kuhl House Poets

David Micah Greenberg
Planned Solstice

John Isles
Ark

John Isles
Inverse Sky

Bin Ramke
Airs, Waters, Places

Bin Ramke
Matter

Michelle Robinson
The Life of a Hunter

Robyn Schiff
Revolver

Robyn Schiff
Worth

Rod Smith
Deed

Cole Swensen
The Book of a Hundred Hands

Cole Swensen
Such Rich Hour

Tony Tost
Complex Sleep

Emily Wilson
The Keep